Vegan Dinner Recipes
50 Delicious Vegan Dinner Recipes For Every Occasion

By Jessica Brooks

© Copyright 2015 by Jessica Brooks - All rights reserved.

This document is geared towards providing exact and reliable information in regards to the topic and issue covered. The publication is sold with the idea that the publisher is not required to render accounting, officially permitted, or otherwise, qualified services. If advice is necessary, legal or professional, a practiced individual in the profession should be ordered.

- From a Declaration of Principles which was accepted and approved equally by a Committee of the American Bar Association and a Committee of Publishers and Associations.

In no way is it legal to reproduce, duplicate, or transmit any part of this document in either electronic means or in printed format. Recording of this publication is strictly prohibited and any storage of this document is not allowed unless with written permission from the publisher. All rights reserved.

The information provided herein is stated to be truthful and consistent, in that any liability, in terms of inattention or otherwise, by any usage or abuse of any policies, processes, or directions contained within is the solitary and utter responsibility of the recipient reader. Under no circumstances will any legal responsibility or blame be held against the publisher for any reparation, damages, or monetary loss due to the information herein, either directly or indirectly.

Respective authors own all copyrights not held by the publisher.

The information herein is offered for informational purposes solely, and is universal as so. The presentation of the information is without contract or any type of guarantee assurance.

The trademarks that are used are without any consent, and the publication of the trademark is without permission or backing by the trademark owner. All trademarks and brands within this book are for clarifying purposes only and are the owned by the owners themselves, not affiliated with this document.

Disclaimer – Please read!

The information provided in this book is designed to provide helpful information on the subjects discussed. This book is not meant to be used, nor should it be used, to diagnose or treat any medical condition. For diagnosis or treatment of any medical problem, consult your own physician. The publisher and author are not responsible for any specific health or allergy needs that may require medical supervision and are not liable for any damages or negative consequences from any treatment, action, application or preparation, to any person reading or following the information in this book. References are provided for informational purposes only and do not constitute endorsement of any websites or other sources. Readers should be aware that the websites listed in this book may change.

Table of Contents

Introduction 7
Say Yes to Your New Lifestyle 8
What Everybody Should Know about Vegan Diet? 10
How this cookbook can come in handy? 11
Herb-Roasted Yukon Potatoes with Carrots 12
Creamy Smashed Potatoes with Spinach 13
Quinoa Pilaf with Pistachios and Carrots 14
Grandma's Eggplant with Lentils 15
Sunday Spiced Rice and Beans 17
Creamy Cheesy Pasta with Cashews 18
Nutty Rice with Beans 20
Creamy Country Noodles with Mushrooms 22
Amazing Coconut Sugar Snap Peas 24
Easy and Healthy Mexican Quinoa 25
Gnocchi with Herbed Tomato Sauce 26
Saucy Spaghetti with Beans 28
Country Veggie Pie 30
Amazing Italian Stuffed Peppers 32
Quick Herbed Beans with Pasta 34
Mom's Chili Beans 35
Creamy Mushroom Lasagna 37
Eggplant Lasagna with Tofu Ricotta 39
Slow Cooker Vegetable Stew 40
Vegetable Coconut Sunday Chili 41
Winter Barley and Vegetable Chili 42
Super Creamy Baked Macaroni 43
Quick and Easy Seitan Crumbles 44
Meat-Free BBQ Sandwiches 45
Vegetable Curry Delight 46
Slow Cooker Sweet Potatoes 47
Smoked Lentil Sandwiches 48
Smoked Breaded Tofu Sticks 49
Mexican-Style Arepas Horneadas 50
Meatless Sizzling Fajitas 52
Potato Curry with Beans 54
Chickpea Vegetable Stir-Fry 55
Perfect Shepherd's Pie 57
Flavor-Rich Crusty Tart 59

5

Nutty Mushroom Tofu Casserole 61
Apple Gourmet Sausages 63
Amazing Sandwiches with Pumpkin Sausages 64
Homemade Meatless Frankfurters 66
Savory Vegetable Muffins 67
Creamy Bean and Tomato Soup 69
Saucy Tofu with Vegetables 70
Mushroom and Carrot Stuffed Zucchini 71
Mexican-Style Macaroni Skillet 73
Herbed and Stewed Summer Vegetables 74
Tangy BBQ Sandwiches with Tempeh 75
Colorful Mushroom Vegetable Pilaf 76
Mediterranean Veggie Couscous 77
Easy Portobello Mushroom Pasta 79
Super Healthy Vegetable Rice Stew 81
Peppery Seitan Fajitas 83
Free Ebook Offer 84
About the Author 85
Valerian Press 86
Free Preview of "Vegan Slow Cooker Cookbook: 100 Delicious Recipes" 87

Introduction

Those who choose to follow a vegan diet and animal-free lifestyle do this for quite a number of reasons. Some of the reasons include health empowerment, animal compassion, environmental issues, religious reasons, etc. You could possibly just want to minimize consumption of meat and meat products. Maybe you are considering making the switch to a vegan diet and you haven't a clue about what to do for the beginning. Maybe a member of your family or your close friend made the decision to become a vegan, therefore you are keen to show your full support. No matter what your reason, make sure that the reason is strong enough and clear enough in order to persist with your intention. Ultimately, the reason may be very simple, as George Bernard Shaw, a famous Irish playwright, said, "Animals are my friends...and I don't eat my friends."

Regardless of whether you are an absolute beginner or you are an experienced long-time vegan, this cookbook come in handy when you want to enrich your menu and surprise your guests.

Say Yes to Your New Lifestyle

A vegan lifestyle is not just a matter of food and refraining from eating food of animal origin. Most vegans do not wear animal based products such as wool, leather, fur, and so on. Most vegans also do not use beauty products which contain some animal derivatives. It is important to point out that the well-planned vegan diet is a marathon, not a sprint. Why, in fact, go vegan?

There are a lot of health benefits to going vegan.

1) **Prevention and healing.** Vegan diet can help in the prevention of a number of diseases such as diabetes, cancer, arthritis, cardiovascular disease, osteoporosis, etc. Moreover, you can solve your problems with migraine, excess weight, allergies, PMS symptoms, skin condition, and so on. At the same time, you can improve your mental health, knowing what you are doing for yourself and other living beings. Your adventure towards effective mind-body healing is determined by a methodical step-by-step process. You will see, going vegan will intrigue you to learn more about food and nutrition. The more you learn, the more you will be able to overcome a variety of health problems, while improving your well-being. Anyway, if you are suffering from any health problem, please consult your physician or a registered dietitian.
2) **Nutritional benefits.** Vegan diet is rich in foods such as fresh vegetables and fruits, nuts, whole grains and so on. These foods are high in vitamins and minerals, as well as fiber, antioxidants, good carbs, proteins, and fats.
3) **Physical Benefits.** Eating vegan helps you to have more energy for your daily activities, whereby you feel much stronger and more mobile. You might have heard about vegan weight loss diet. Many studies have shown that a plant-based diet has a very positive effect on weight loss. When you avoid harmful products such as saturated fat and sugar, you can reduce your weight in a natural and healthy way.

In addition to the previously mentioned reasons, there are a number of other very significant reasons. There are an issue of global food supply, environmental protection, the risk of salmonella infection and the risk of E. coli from animal products and so on. Nonetheless, farm animals are given hormones and antibiotics which further increases the risks for human health. For many responsible people, it is a hard pill to swallow and they become vegans.

Therefore, veganism is more than just a way of eating. This is a profound attitude towards life and responsibility for the survival of our planet.

What Everybody Should Know about Vegan Diet?

First of all, do not make the switch to a vegan diet at once. If you are meat eater your whole life, do not expect to become a vegan overnight. Slow down and be patient. Gradually and slowly remove certain food groups from your diet, one at a time. What else should you know?

- **Your protein sources.** When some people exclude the food of animal origin, how can they get necessary proteins? As a matter of fact, all plants contain protein. However, the best vegan sources of protein are almonds, banana, brown rice, tofu, beans, whole wheat bread, quinoa, soy milk and many others.
- **Healthy vegans vs. Junk vegans.** Do not replace animal products with snacks, sweets, junk food, and soft drinks. Make better and healthier choices and stay away from junk food. This should mean that you need to cook at home as much as you can. With the assistance of a good cookbook, it will not be difficult at all.
- **Vitamin B12.** Keep in mind that vitamin B12 is found in meat and eggs. Therefore, you need to find a good B12 supplement.
- **The cost of being vegan**. With a dash of cleverness, you can go vegan on a budget. Here are a few tips: cook at home, buy food in bulk, freeze your leftovers, buy local and seasonal fruits and vegetables. And here is the best one – bypassing the butcher shop, you can save your money for sure.

How this cookbook can come in handy?

Nutrient-rich diet. Things are not as simple as it seems. As a vegan, you have to be sure that you are getting necessary nutritional ingredients. Each of your meals should be well-balanced. There is no need to worry, each recipe in this cookbook is carefully selected and adjusted to the nutritional needs of the average adult. This cookbook consist of fifty delicious main course recipes. You will have complete information about meal preparation, including preparation time, serving size, ingredients, and directions.

Weight Loss. We are aware that it is not easy, therefore many people drop by the wayside. You might have tried everything, but you did not see results. Give a vegan diet a try. This book can help you to prepare meals that are finger licking good so you will not have the feeling that you renounce your favorite foods. If you intend to lose weight, simply reduce the portions and you will no longer crave unhealthy food that make you fat. Feel free to minimize the amount of fat that is specified in the recipe.

Cooking can be very exciting. Please keep in mind that no one is born a good cook. You cannot be bothered cooking or you just have no time to cook. This cookbook contains brilliant ideas to make cooking interesting and easy. Meat and dairy substitutes can make a big difference. You will be surprised how tasty and imaginative these meals are!

These are delicious savory recipes that you can serve to anyone, regardless of whether or not they are eating vegan. Grab your pan and let's cook!

Herb-Roasted Yukon Potatoes with Carrots

(Ready in about 1 hour | Servings 4)

Ingredients

- 2 tablespoons canola oil
- 1 tablespoon yellow mustard
- 1 teaspoon sea salt
- 1/4 teaspoon ground black pepper
- 1/4 teaspoon cayenne pepper
- 2 cloves garlic, minced
- 1 teaspoon dried basil
- 1 teaspoon dried rosemary, crumbled
- 1/4 cup dry white wine
- 1 ¼ pounds baby Yukon potatoes, thoroughly washed, scrubbed, and halved
- 1/2 pound baby carrots, halved
- 2-3 spring onions, sliced

Directions

1. Preheat the oven to 400 degrees F. Prepare a suitable 8-inch baking dish.
2. In a bowl, combine oil, yellow mustard, salt, black pepper, cayenne, garlic, basil, rosemary, and dry white wine. Then, stir to combine and transfer to the baking dish.
3. Next, add the potatoes, carrots and onions to the baking dish.
4. Cover the dish with a foil and bake approximately 30 minutes.
5. Remove the foil and stir gently. Continue baking until the potatoes are fork-tender, or approximately 20 to 25 minutes. Serve immediately and enjoy!

Creamy Smashed Potatoes with Spinach
(Ready in about 40 minutes | Servings 6)

Ingredients

- 1 pound frozen spinach
- 2 ½ pounds potatoes
- 3 tablespoons Dijon mustard
- 1/4 cup margarine
- 1/4 cup non-dairy sour cream
- 1 teaspoon garlic powder
- 1 teaspoon seasoned salt
- 1/4 teaspoon ground black pepper
- 1 teaspoon dried basil

Directions

1. Cook the spinach according to the package instructions. Drain and reserve, keeping it warm.
2. Meanwhile, peel the potatoes. Next, cut the potatoes into bite-sized chunks. In a pot, boil potato chunks in a salted water until fork-tender. Drain the potato chunks and return to the pot.
3. Add the cooked spinach and remaining ingredients to the pot. Mash ingredients until the mixture is uniform and creamy, or until your desired consistency is reached. Serve immediately.

Quinoa Pilaf with Pistachios and Carrots

(Ready in about 20 minutes | Servings 2)

Ingredients

- 1 cup quinoa, rinsed and drained
- 2 tablespoons vegetable olive oil
- 2 tablespoons apple cider vinegar
- 1 teaspoon kosher salt, to taste
- 1/2 teaspoon ground black pepper
- 1 clove garlic, minced
- 3 tablespoon scallions, chopped
- 1 tablespoon fresh parsley, chopped
- 1 teaspoon ginger root, grated
- 1/2 teaspoon ground cumin
- 1/2 pistachios toasted
- 1 handful fresh cilantro, chopped
- 1 carrot, grated

Directions

1. Pour water into a deep saucepan and bring to a boil. Then, turn the heat to medium and cook the quinoa until it softens or for 10 minutes.
2. Next, drain cooked quinoa, fluffing with a fork and set aside.
3. In a large bowl, whisk the oil, vinegar, salt, pepper, garlic, scallions, parsley, grated ginger, and cumin. Mix well to combine.
4. Next, stir in reserved quinoa and pistachios. Scatter with the cilantro and grated carrot over the top and serve.

Grandma's Eggplant with Lentils

(Ready in about 20 minutes | Servings 2)

Ingredients

- 1 eggplant
- 1 tablespoon sesame oil
- 1 teaspoon sea salt
- 2 cloves garlic, minced
- 1 small yellow onion, finely chopped
- 1 teaspoon ground cumin
- 1/4 teaspoon red pepper, crushed
- 1/4 teaspoon ground black pepper
- 1 cup cooked lentils, rinsed
- 2 ½ cups water
- 1 tablespoon soy sauce
- 1 tablespoon vegan Worcestershire sauce
- 1 tablespoon fresh parsley, for garnish

Directions

1. Partially peel the eggplant and then cut it into thin pieces. In a large heavy skillet, heat the sesame oil over medium-high flame. Add prepared eggplant slices and season them with sea salt. Cook about 10 minutes, until the eggplant slices have browned.
2. Stir in the minced garlic and onions and cook 2 more minutes.
3. Then, add cumin, red pepper, black pepper and lentils. Cook for a minute longer.
4. Pour in the water and stir to combine ingredients. Add soy sauce, Worcestershire sauce and then bring it to a boil.
5. Cover, turn the heat to low, and simmer, until the lentil is tender and the water is absorbed, about 25 minutes. Stir occasionally.
6. Transfer your meal to a nice serving bowl, sprinkle with prepared parsley and serve with your favorite salad!

Sunday Spiced Rice and Beans

(Ready in about 55 minutes | Servings 8)

Ingredients

- 2 tablespoons canola oil
- 2 carrots, sliced
- 2 stalks celery, chopped
- 1/2 jalapeño pepper, minced
- 1 red bell pepper, seeded and diced
- 1 cup onions, chopped
- 1 teaspoon salt
- 1/2 teaspoon cayenne pepper
- 1/4 cup tamari sauce
- 2 ¾ cups vegetable broth
- 1 ½ cups long grain white rice
- 1 can (15-ounces) kidney beans

Directions

1. In a large-size pot, heat the canola oil over medium flame.
2. Add the carrots, celery, jalapeño pepper, red bell pepper, onions, salt and cayenne pepper. Then, cover the pot and cook for about 15 minutes, or until the onions are soft and the vegetables are slightly browned.
3. Next, add the tamari sauce and vegetable broth and deglaze your pot. Bring to a boil.
4. Add uncooked rice, bring to a boil again, and then reduce the heat to low.
5. Continue simmering for about 20 minutes. Drain the kidney beans, but do not rinse them. Then, add the beans to the pot and cook until the mixture is heated through. Serve!

Creamy Cheesy Pasta with Cashews
(Ready in about 35 minutes | Servings 4)

Ingredients

- 1 ½ cup eggless pasta of choice
- 2 cups non-dairy milk
- 1/2 cup non-dairy cream cheese
- 3 tablespoons cashews, chopped
- 3 tablespoons nutritional yeast
- 1 teaspoon sea salt
- 1/4 teaspoon cayenne pepper
- 1/4 teaspoon freshly ground black pepper
- 2 tablespoons extra-virgin olive oil
- 2 cloves garlic, minced
- 1/4 cup fresh parsley
- 1 tablespoon fresh cilantro
- Tomato ketchup for garnish (optional)

Directions

1. In a pot, cook the eggless pasta according to directions on a package. Drain the pasta, reserving 1/2 cup of the pasta cooking water.
2. Add the milk, cream cheese, cashews, nutritional yeast, salt, cayenne pepper and ground black pepper to a food

processor or a blender. Process until the mixture is uniform and smooth.
3. In a cast-iron skillet, heat the oil over medium heat. Next, sauté the garlic, stirring constantly, about a minute. Add the cashew mixture and 1/2 cup of the reserved water. Bring it to a simmer and continue cooking until it becomes creamy and thick, approximately 8 minutes.
4. Remove the skillet from the heat and add the pasta. Stir in the parsley and cilantro and toss to combine.
5. Divide the pasta among four serving plates and serve with ketchup.

Nutty Rice with Beans

(Ready in about 1 hour | Servings 4)

Ingredients

- 1 tablespoon olive oil
- 1 clove garlic, minced
- 1 ¼ cups brown rice
- 2 ½ cups water
- 1 bay leaf
- 1 teaspoon Himalayan salt
- 1/2 teaspoon black pepper
- 1/2 teaspoon red pepper flakes, crushed
- 1 tablespoon fresh parsley, chopped
- 1 tablespoon fresh cilantro, chopped
- 1 can (15-ounces) Great Northern beans
- 1/3 cup almond, roughly chopped
- 2 tablespoons margarine, softened
- 2 cups red onion, finely chopped
- 1 Roma tomato, diced
- 1 teaspoon lemon zest

Directions

1. In a wok or a large and wide saucepan, heat the oil over medium flame. Then, add garlic and rice, and stir-fry for 2 to 3 minutes.
2. Add the water, bay leaf and 1/2 teaspoon of the salt. Then, bring to a boil, cover with the lid, and simmer about 45 minutes, or until the rice becomes soft.
3. Reduce the heat to low. Add the black pepper, red pepper, parsley and cilantro. Drain and rinse the beans and add them to the pan along with chopped almonds. Stir to combine ingredients and reserve.
4. In a separate saucepan or a wok, melt the softened margarine. Sauté the onions until tender and translucent or about 5 minutes. Add remaining 1/2 teaspoon of salt and stir to combine.

5. Add the tomato and lemon zest, and continue cooking for 2 to 3 more minutes. Pour this tomato mixture into rice mixture. Cook until heated through. Serve warm.

Creamy Country Noodles with Mushrooms

(Ready in about 45 minutes | Servings 6)

Ingredients

- 1 cup uncooked vegan noodles
- 1 tablespoon sesame oil
- 3-4 green onions, sliced
- 3 tablespoons all-purpose flour
- 2 cups vegetable broth
- 1 tablespoon tomato paste
- 1 ½ pounds button mushrooms, sliced
- 1/2 teaspoon seasoned salt
- 1/4 teaspoon ground black pepper
- 1/2 teaspoon garlic powder
- 1/2 teaspoon dried thyme
- 1 tablespoon fresh rosemary
- 1 teaspoon dried basil
- 1 tablespoon apple cider vinegar

Directions

1. Prepare the noodles according to the directions on the package until they are al dente. Set aside and cover, keeping the noodles warm.
2. In a wok or a large skillet, heat the oil over medium flame. Sauté the green onions until soft and translucent, or for 3 minutes. Add the flour and cook for 30 seconds, stirring often.
3. Gradually add the vegetable broth and tomato paste, stirring constantly. Continue to stir for about 1 minute until this mixture becomes bubbly.
4. Next, add the mushrooms, seasoned salt, black pepper, garlic powder, thyme, rosemary, and basil. Stir to combine ingredients.
5. Continue cooking for 5 minutes, until the mushrooms are tender and fragrant.

6. Add the apple cider vinegar. Turn the heat to low and cook for 4 more minutes. Finally add cooked noodles and gently stir to combine. Serve immediately.

Amazing Coconut Sugar Snap Peas

(Ready in about 45 minutes | Servings 6)

Ingredients

- 14 ounces water
- 1 can (14-ounce) coconut milk
- 2 cups uncooked wild rice
- 3 tablespoons fresh lemon juice
- 1/2 teaspoon sea salt
- 1/4 teaspoon ground black pepper
- 1 teaspoon dried basil
- 2 tablespoons sesame seeds, toasted
- 6 ounces raw sugar snap peas

Directions

1. In a large saucepan or a wok, combine the water, coconut milk and rice. Then bring to a boil.
2. Turn the heat to low. Continue simmering, covered, for about 20 minutes.
3. Remove the pan from the flame, remove the lid, and then add the lemon juice, salt, pepper and dried basil.
4. Fold in the sesame seeds and sugar snap peas. Stir to combine and enjoy warm or cold.

Easy and Healthy Mexican Quinoa
(Ready in about 35 minutes | Servings 10)

Ingredients

- 4 cups water
- 2 cups white quinoa
- 1 can (15-ounces) red kidney beans, drained and rinsed
- 2 cups corn kernels
- 1 cup chunky salsa
- 2 tablespoons extra-virgin olive oil
- 1 tablespoon lime zest
- 1 bay leaf
- Sea salt to taste
- 6-7 black peppercorns
- 1 teaspoon cayenne pepper
- 1 teaspoon dried basil
- 1 tablespoon fresh cilantro, chopped

Directions

1. In a large pot, bring the water to a boil. Add the quinoa, bring to a boil, then lower the heat, cover and continue cooking, for about 10 minutes, or until all of the liquid has been absorbed.
2. Remove the pot from the heat. Fluff cooked quinoa with a fork, and allow to rest for about 10 minutes in order to cool slightly.
3. Meanwhile, combine remaining ingredients in a large-size bowl.
4. Next, stir in the quinoa. Stir to combine ingredients. Serve with your favorite veggies such as tomato, bell pepper and onion. Serve hot or at room temperature, it's up to you.

Gnocchi with Herbed Tomato Sauce
(Ready in about 1 hour 45 minutes | Servings 4)

Ingredients

For the gnocchi:

- 1 pound fingerling potatoes
- 2 tablespoons canola oil
- 1 cup all-purpose flour, plus more for dusting
- 1/2 teaspoon dried oregano
- 1/2 teaspoon dried basil
- 1 teaspoon garlic powder
- 1 teaspoon Kosher salt
- 1/4 teaspoon ground black pepper
- 1/4 teaspoon red pepper flakes

For the Sauce:

- 1 teaspoon extra-virgin olive oil
- 1 small onion, chopped
- 2 cloves garlic, minced
- 4 large tomatoes, diced
- 1/2 teaspoon salt
- 1/4 teaspoon black pepper
- 1/4 teaspoon cayenne pepper
- 1 teaspoon dried rosemary
- 1/2 teaspoon dried basil
- 1/2 teaspoon dried oregano

Directions

1. To make the gnocchi, preheat the oven 400 degrees F.
2. Prick a few holes in the potatoes with a fork. Place potatoes in a roasting pan and bake them for about 1 hour. Allow the potatoes to cool completely.
3. Discard the skins from the potatoes and add canola. Then mash the potatoes in a large bowl.

4. Add remaining ingredients for the gnocchi. Knead the batter until it is elastic and soft. Place the batter on a well-floured surface. Divide the batter into 4 equal balls.
5. Next, roll each ball into a rope and cut each rope into 12 equal pieces.
6. Bring a pot of water to a boil and cook the gnocchi until they float to the top of the water.
7. To make the sauce, in a heavy skillet, heat the oil. Sauté the onions and garlic until they are tender and fragrant.
8. Then add remaining ingredients for the sauce and cook for about 15 minutes, stirring occasionally.
9. Divide the gnocchi among four serving plates, spoon the sauce onto the pasta and serve.

Saucy Spaghetti with Beans

(Ready in about 30 minutes | Servings 4)

Ingredients

- 1 tablespoon sesame oil
- 1/2 cup scallions
- 2 cloves garlic, minced
- 1 zucchini, grated
- 1/4 cup dried cranberries
- 2 teaspoons ground cumin
- 1 teaspoon cayenne pepper
- 1 teaspoon ground ginger
- 1 can (15-ounces) cannellini beans, drained and rinsed
- 1 can (15-ounce) tomato sauce
- 1/2 cup eggless spaghetti of choice
- 1 cup water
- 1/2 teaspoon kosher salt
- 2 tablespoon fresh parsley, chopped
- Kalamata olives for garnish

Directions

1. In a large-size saucepan, heat the sesame oil over medium-high flame. Then sauté the scallions, garlic, grated zucchini, and cranberries. Cook until the vegetables are tender, about 4 minutes.
2. Add the cumin, cayenne, ginger, and cook until fragrant, or for 1 minute.
3. Stir in the beans and tomato sauce, add the spaghetti and water. Add salt and stir well to combine.
4. Turn the heat to low and simmer for 15 minutes, stirring occasionally to prevent spaghetti from sticking to the bottom of the pot. Cook until the spaghetti are al dente.
5. Divide the spaghetti among four serving plates, sprinkle parsley on top and garnish with Kalamata olives. Enjoy!

Country Veggie Pie

(Ready in about 2 hours 20 minutes | Servings 4)

Ingredients

For the crust:

- 1/4 cup hot water (100 degrees F)
- 1 teaspoons active dry yeast
- 1 tablespoon molasses
- 2 ½ cups whole-wheat flour, plus more for dusting
- 1 teaspoon kosher salt
- 1/2 cup salsa
- 1 ½ tablespoon olive oil

For the filling:

- 1 teaspoon olive oil
- 6 ounces soy chorizo
- 2 cloves garlic, grated
- 1/4 cup leeks, chopped
- 1 1/3 cup frozen green peas
- 1 cup salsa, store-bought or homemade

Directions

1. To make the crust, in a small bowl, combine the water, yeast and molasses. Stir to combine and let stand for about 10 minutes, until the yeast is completely dissolved.
2. In a large bowl, stir together the whole-wheat flour, kosher salt, salsa, and 1 tablespoon of the olive oil.
3. Add the dissolved yeast to the flour mixture and stir to combine. Transfer this mixture to a floured surface. Then, knead your dough 10 to 12 minutes, or until the dough is smooth and elastic.
4. Shape your dough into a large ball. Brush the ball of dough with the remaining ½ tablespoon of olive oil. Allow your dough to rise until it is double in size, or for about 90 minutes.

5. Meanwhile, make the filling. In a large heavy skillet, heat the olive oil. Then, crumble the soy chorizo into the skillet. Add the garlic and leeks. Cook over medium heat about 5 minutes.
6. Add the peas and salsa, lower the heat and simmer for 6 more minutes.
7. Preheat the oven to 375 degrees F. Coat a baking sheet with parchment paper or Silpat.
8. Punch airy, risen dough. Roll the dough out and shape it into an 8 × 10-inch rectangle on the coated baking sheet. Place the filling evenly on top and allow to rest for approximately 20 minutes.
9. Bake until the edges of the pie are golden brown, 20 to 25 minutes. Allow the pie to cool slightly before cutting and serving.

Amazing Italian Stuffed Peppers

(Ready in about 1 hour | Servings 4)

Ingredients

- 4 medium red bell peppers
- 2 tablespoons canola oil
- 1 onion, chopped
- 2 clove garlic, minced
- 2 small zucchini, grated
- 1 ½ cups mushrooms, sliced
- 1 teaspoon cumin
- 1 tablespoon chili powder
- 1 teaspoon paprika
- 1 tablespoon fresh cilantro, roughly chopped
- 1 tablespoon fresh parsley, roughly chopped
- 2 cups whole-wheat breadcrumbs
- 1/2 cup vegan Parmesan cheese
- 1 teaspoon kosher salt
- 1/2 teaspoon ground black pepper

Directions

1. Core peppers, then discard seeds and all the white pith. Wash the peppers and then parboil them in boiling water for 3 minutes.
2. The peppers should stand upright in a baking dish, so, if necessary, cut a very small slice off the bottom of the pepper. Then rinse under the cold, running water, drain and set aside.
3. To make the filling: In a large heavy skillet, heat canola oil. Sauté the onion and garlic for about 2 minutes, stirring often. Add grated zucchini and cook another 3 minutes.
4. Next, add mushrooms and sauté another 1 to 2 minutes. Finally, add the rest of ingredients and cook for a few minutes longer, until the mixture is heated through.
5. Stuff prepared bell peppers with the filling. Arrange the stuffed peppers in the baking dish and bake at 350

degrees F for about 40 minutes. Enjoy immediately with your favorite vegan salad!

Quick Herbed Beans with Pasta

(Ready in about 20 minutes | Servings 3)

Ingredients

- 1 tablespoon olive oil
- 1 red onion, finely chopped
- 2 cloves garlic, minced
- 1/2 cup pecans, halved
- 1 (15-ounce) can kidney beans
- 1 bay leaf
- 1 teaspoon dried basil
- 1 tablespoon fresh sage
- 1 teaspoon dried thyme
- 1/4 teaspoon ground black pepper
- 1/4 teaspoon paprika
- 6 ounces cooked eggless pasta

Directions

1. In a wide saucepan, heat the oil and sauté the onion and garlic for a few minutes, until the onion is tender and fragrant. Add pecans and sauté for a few more minutes.
2. Drain the beans, reserving a small amount of the juice.
3. Add the beans to the saucepan, and cook, so the flavors can blend.
4. Next, add reserved juice, the spices and herbs and stir to combine. Cook until the beans are heated through.
5. Serve with your favorite eggless pasta, but any vegan salad might also work.

Mom's Chili Beans
(Ready in about 1 hour 15 minutes | Servings 6)

Ingredients

- 1 tablespoon extra-virgin olive oil
- 2 tablespoons dry sherry
- 2 medium-size red onions, finely chopped
- 1 cup carrots, chopped
- 1 red bell pepper, thinly sliced
- 4 cups brown beans, cooked
- 1 cup water
- 1 cup vegetable broth
- 2 cloves fresh garlic, minced
- 1 large tomato
- 1 teaspoon celery seeds
- 1 teaspoon saffron
- 1 tablespoon chili powder
- 1/4 cup fresh cilantro, chopped
- 1 teaspoon agave nectar
- 1 teaspoon sea salt
- 4-5 black peppercorns
- Tortilla chips, crushed

Directions

1. In a large stockpot, heat the oil and dry sherry over medium flame.
2. Sauté the onions approximately 8 minutes. Stir in carrots and bell pepper and continue cooking another 5 minutes, stirring constantly. Add beans and stir to combine.
3. Next, add water, broth, garlic, tomato, celery seeds, saffron, chili powder, cilantro, agave nectar, sea salt, and peppercorns, and bring to a boil.
4. Cover with the lid, turn the heat to low and simmer for about 1 hour. Serve with crushed tortilla chips.

Creamy Mushroom Lasagna

(Ready in about 1 hour 30 minutes | Servings 6)

Ingredients

- 2 tablespoons margarine or non-dairy butter
- 2 cloves garlic, minced
- 1 pound mushrooms, sliced
- 2 cups unsweetened soy milk
- 1/4 cup nutritional yeast
- 1 teaspoon dried oregano
- 1 tablespoon dried basil
- 1/2 teaspoon sea salt
- 1/4 teaspoon ground black pepper
- 1/2 cup all-purpose flour
- 12 lasagna noodles, prepared according to package directions
- 2 cups Tofu Ricotta

Directions

1. Preheat the oven to 350 degrees F. Have ready a suitable casserole dish.
2. In a medium-size skillet, melt the margarine or butter over medium-high heat. Then, add the minced garlic with mushrooms. Sauté until the mushrooms are tender and fragrant, for 5 minutes.
3. Add the soy milk, yeast, oregano, basil, salt, and pepper. Bring to a boil. Then lower the heat and simmer for 15 more minutes.
4. Combine the flour with 1/2 cup water to make a slurry. Slowly add the flour slurry and cook until it is thickened. Remove from the heat.
5. To make the lasagna: Place a thin layer of mushroom mixture in the bottom of the casserole dish. Then, lay 3 noodles, then place a thin layer of mushroom mixture, and finally place a layer of ricotta. Repeat until you run out of ingredients.

6. Cover and bake in preheated oven approximately 25 minutes. Uncover and bake for another 15 minutes.
7. Let the lasagna stand for at least 15 minutes before cutting and serving.

Eggplant Lasagna with Tofu Ricotta

(Ready in about 1 hour 10 minutes | Servings 12)

Ingredients

- 2 eggplants, thinly sliced
- 2 ¼ cups marinara sauce
- 2 tablespoon fresh cilantro, chopped
- 2 tablespoon fresh parsley, chopped
- 1 tablespoon dried basil
- 1 teaspoon dried oregano
- 2 cups Tofu Ricotta
- 6 medium-size tomatoes, thinly sliced

Directions

1. Preheat the oven to 350 degrees F. Prepare a 9×13-inch baking dish.
2. In the bottom of the baking dish, place a thin layer of marinara sauce. Then, arrange the eggplant slices in a single layer. Again, place the marinara sauce over the eggplant. Sprinkle fresh cilantro over the eggplant slices.
3. Scatter Tofu ricotta in a thin layer. Sprinkle the parsley, basil and oregano over it. Add a single layer of tomato slices over the Tofu ricotta. Repeat this process with remaining ingredients. Finally, you will have 4 layers.
4. Cover with an aluminum foil and bake the lasagna for 30 minutes. Then, remove the foil and bake for 20 more minutes.
5. Allow to stand for about 15 minutes before cutting and serving.

Slow Cooker Vegetable Stew
(Ready in about 4 hours 5 minutes | Servings 8)

Ingredients

- 1 tablespoon canola oil
- 3 garlic cloves, minced
- 1 onion, thinly sliced
- 2 medium potatoes, diced
- 1 tablespoon kosher salt
- 1 teaspoon celery seeds
- 1 tablespoon grated ginger
- 1/4 teaspoon paprika
- 1 cup vegetable stock
- 1 cup water
- 2 bay leaves
- 2 (15.5-ounce) cans chickpeas, drained and rinsed
- 1 red bell pepper, diced
- 1 medium head of broccoli, broken into florets
- 1 (28-ounce) can tomatoes with juice
- 1/4 teaspoon ground black pepper

Directions

1. In a saucepan, heat the canola oil over medium flame. Sauté the garlic and onion until translucent and fragrant, for 5 minutes. Add the potatoes and cook for a few more minutes.
2. Add the salt, celery seeds, grated ginger, paprika, and cook an additional 30 seconds to 1 minute. Pour in vegetable stock and stir well to combine. Transfer this mixture to a slow cooker.
3. Add the rest of ingredients, stir to combine ingredients. Then, cover and cook for 4 hours on high. Serve hot with your favorite ciabatta rolls, if desired.

Vegetable Coconut Sunday Chili

(Ready in about 8 hours | Servings 8)

Ingredients

- 1/2 cup leeks, finely chopped
- 2 carrots, peeled and chopped
- 1/2 cup celery stalks, chopped
- 1 plum tomato, chopped
- 2 cups butternut squash, diced
- 3 large cloves garlic, minced
- 1 medium can of red beans, drained and rinsed
- 1 medium can of chickpeas, drained and rinsed
- 1 can non-dairy milk
- 2 teaspoons chili powder
- 1 teaspoon dried basil
- 1 tablespoon dried sage
- 2 cups vegetable broth
- 1/2 teaspoon kosher salt
- 1/2 teaspoon cayenne pepper
- 5-6 black peppercorns
- Chopped fresh chives, for garnish

Directions

1. Place all ingredients except the chives in a crock pot. Cook the chili on low heat for 8 hours.
2. In the last 1 hour of cooking, uncover the pot to allow the chili to thicken.
3. Divide among serving plates, scatter the chives over the top of chili and serve.

Winter Barley and Vegetable Chili

(Ready in about 55 minutes | Servings 4)

Ingredients

- 1 tablespoon olive oil
- 1 zucchini, finely diced
- 1 carrot, finely diced
- 2 cloves garlic, minced
- 1 large-size onions
- 1/2 teaspoon sea salt
- 2 tablespoons chili powder
- 1/2 teaspoon smoked paprika
- 1 teaspoon celery seeds
- 1 tablespoon dried basil
- 1 cup uncooked pearl barley, drained
- 3 cups vegetable broth
- 1 can (15-ounce) tomato sauce
- 1 can (15-ounces) pinto beans, cooked, drained and rinsed

Directions

1. In a deep and wide saucepan, heat the oil over medium-high heat. Stir in the zucchini, carrot, garlic, onion, and salt and reduce the heat to medium. Cook for 5 minutes.
2. Next, add the chili powder, paprika, celery seeds, and basil. Cook for 1 minute longer.
3. Add the barley, and cook an additional 2 minutes.
4. Add the broth and tomato sauce, and stir well to combine. Bring to a boil. Turn the heat to low, cover with the lid and simmer for 35 minutes, stirring occasionally.
5. Uncover the saucepan and stir in the beans. Continue cooking for 10 minutes over the low heat and serve warm.

Super Creamy Baked Macaroni

(Ready in about 1 hour 15 minutes | Servings 4)

Ingredients

- Nonstick cooking spray
- 8 ounces whole-grain macaroni

For the topping:

- 1 cup bread crumbs
- 1/2 teaspoon kosher salt
- 1/2 teaspoon dried oregano
- 1 teaspoon dried basil
- 1 teaspoon dried rosemary
- 2 tablespoons extra-virgin olive oil

For the sauce:

- 1 cup nutritional yeast
- 2 tablespoons all-purpose flour
- 1 teaspoon onion powder
- 1 teaspoon garlic powder
- 1 teaspoon ground cumin
- 1 teaspoon kosher salt
- 2 cups unsweetened soy milk
- 1 tablespoon tahini
- 2 tablespoons margarine

Directions

1. Preheat the oven to 375 degrees F. Oil a baking dish with nonstick cooking spray.
2. Cook the macaroni following the package directions. Drain the macaroni, reserving 1/2 cup of the liquid.
3. To make the topping: In a bowl, combine all of the ingredients for the topping and stir well to combine. Set aside.
4. To make the sauce: In a saucepan, combine the nutritional yeast, flour, onion powder, garlic powder,

cumin, kosher salt, soy milk and tahini. Cook over medium-high heat, whisking frequently, until your sauce thickens.
5. Whisk in the margarine and stir to combine. Place the sauce, cooked macaroni and reserved liquid in the baking dish and stir to combine.
6. Spread the topping over the pasta and cover with an aluminum foil.
7. Bake in preheated oven for 20 minutes. Next, remove the aluminum foil and continue baking for 10 more minutes. Allow to stand for 10 minutes before cutting and serving.

Quick and Easy Seitan Crumbles
(Ready in about 20 minutes | Servings 2)

Ingredients

- 1/2 cup vital wheat gluten flour
- 2 tablespoons nutritional yeast
- 1 teaspoon agave nectar
- 2 tablespoons tamari sauce
- 1 teaspoon liquid smoke
- 1 tablespoon tomato paste
- 1 tablespoon margarine, melted
- 2 tablespoons water

Directions

1. In a bowl, combine the wheat gluten and nutritional yeast.
2. Stir in the agave nectar, tamari sauce, liquid smoke, tomato paste, margarine, and water. Crumble this mixture.
3. Cook in a saucepan over medium-high heat for 8 minutes.

Meat-Free BBQ Sandwiches

(Ready in about 35 minutes | Servings 6)

Ingredients

- 1 teaspoon extra-virgin olive oil
- 1 cup vital wheat gluten flour
- 1 tablespoon red pepper flakes
- 3 tablespoons nutritional yeast
- 1 teaspoon ground cumin
- 1 teaspoon garlic powder
- 1/4 cup natural peanut butter
- 1 cup water
- 1/2 cup barbecue sauce
- 6 vegan sandwich buns
- Lettuce leaves for garnish

Directions

1. Preheat the oven to 350 degrees F. Lightly grease a rimmed baking sheet with the olive oil.
2. In a large-size bowl, combine the wheat gluten flour, red pepper, nutritional yeast, cumin, and garlic powder. Then stir in the peanut butter and water. Stir until everything is well combined.
3. Divide this mixture into 6 portions. Shape them into 6 strips. Then, place the strips on the baking sheet.
4. Bake for 15 minutes, and then flip the strips and bake on the other side.
5. Drizzle the strips with barbecue sauce and bake for an additional 10 minutes.
6. Then assemble the sandwiches. Divide the strips among 6 sandwich buns, garnish with lettuce leaves and serve.

Vegetable Curry Delight
(Ready in about 30 minutes | Servings 4)

Ingredients

- 1 tablespoon sesame oil
- 1/4 cup scallions, chopped
- 2 cloves garlic, minced
- 1 tablespoon curry powder
- 1 teaspoon turmeric
- 2 teaspoons garam masala
- 1 tablespoon fresh parsley
- 1/2 teaspoon sea salt
- 1 ½ cups soy milk
- 1 tablespoon soy sauce
- 1 head cauliflower, broken into small florets
- 1 head broccoli, broken into small florets
- 15 ounces cooked green beans

Directions

1. In a large-size saucepan or a wok, heat the sesame oil over medium-high heat. Sauté the scallions and garlic until they are fragrant, for about 2 to 3 minutes.
2. Stir in the curry, turmeric, garam masala, parsley, and salt. Cook for 1 minute longer.
3. Pour in the milk and then add the soy sauce. Bring to a boil and add the cauliflower and broccoli. Lower the heat and then simmer for 15 minutes.
4. Add green beans and continue cooking for another 5 to 6 minutes.

Slow Cooker Sweet Potatoes

(Ready in about 4 hours 30 minutes | Servings 4)

Ingredients

- 3 large-size sweet potatoes, diced
- 2 cups water
- 2 cups vegetable stock
- 3-4 spring onions, sliced
- 4 cloves garlic, minced
- 1/2 teaspoon Himalayan salt
- 1 tablespoon chili powder
- 1 tablespoon ground coriander
- 1 ½ cups red lentils
- 1 can non-dairy milk
- Chopped fresh cilantro for garnish

Directions

1. Put the sweet potatoes, water, stock, spring onions, garlic, salt, chili powder and coriander into your slow cooker. Then, cook on high for 3 hours, until the vegetables are just tender.
2. Add the lentils and milk to the slow cooker and stir to combine. Uncover the slow cooker and cook on high for an additional 1½ hours.
3. Sprinkle chopped cilantro on top and serve hot.

Smoked Lentil Sandwiches

(Ready in about 50 minutes | Servings 4)

Ingredients

- 28 ounces canned tomatoes
- 3/4 cup tomato paste
- 1/2 cup blackstrap molasses
- 2 tablespoon dry white wine
- 1 teaspoon lemon zest
- 1 yellow onion, sliced
- 2 tablespoon white vinegar
- 3 garlic cloves
- 1 tablespoon agave nectar
- 1 teaspoon dry mustard
- 1/2 teaspoon Himalayan salt
- 1/4 teaspoon black pepper
- 1/4 teaspoon smoked paprika
- 1/2 teaspoon dried tarragon
- 1/4 teaspoon liquid smoke
- 4 cups cooked lentils
- Vegan salad of choice

Directions

1. Put all of the ingredients, except the cooked lentils and salad, into a blender or a food processor. Process until the mixture is nice, uniform and smooth.
2. Transfer this mixture to a saucepan. Place the lid on the saucepan and bring to a boil over medium-high flame.
3. Next, turn the heat to low and simmer for 30 minutes longer.
4. Remove the saucepan from the heat and stir in lentils. Taste, adjust the seasonings and assemble the sandwiches, garnished with your favorite vegan salad.

Smoked Breaded Tofu Sticks

(Ready in about 30 minutes | Servings 4)

Ingredients

- 1 cup unsweetened soy milk
- 1 cup vegetable broth
- 2 cups smoked extra-firm tofu, pressed
- 3 tablespoons nutritional yeast
- 1 teaspoon salt
- 1/2 teaspoon ground black pepper
- 1 teaspoon dried rosemary
- 1/2 teaspoon paprika
- 1/2 cup all-purpose flour
- Vegetable oil for cooking
- Chopped fresh parsley for garnish

Directions

1. In a bowl, pour in soy milk and vegetable broth.
2. Cut smoked tofu into sticks. Place tofu in a bowl and set aside to soak.
3. To make the breading: In a separate small bowl, stir together yeast, salt, black pepper, rosemary, paprika and flour. Stir until everything is well combined.
4. In a large heavy skillet, warm the oil over medium-high flame.
5. Remove soaked tofu sticks from the bowl and squeeze them. Roll soaked tofu sticks in previously prepared breading.
6. Deep-fry tofu sticks in hot oil until they are crisp and lightly browned. Arrange fried tofu sticks on a serving platter, sprinkle with chopped fresh parsley and serve.

Mexican-Style Arepas Horneadas
(Ready in about 35 minutes | Servings 4)

Ingredients

- Nonstick cooking spray
- 1 cup tofu, drained
- 2 cups prepared polenta
- 2 tablespoons sesame oil
- 2 bananas, sliced
- 1 cup brown beans
- 1 large mango, seeded, and diced
- 1/4 cup scallions, diced
- 1 teaspoon sea salt
- 1/4 teaspoon black pepper
- 1/2 teaspoon paprika
- 1 chili pepper, minced
- 2 avocados, peeled, pitted, and sliced

Directions

1. Preheat the broiler. Grease a baking sheet with nonstick cooking spray.
2. Slice the tofu and polenta into slices similar to cutlets. Brush your slices with 1 tablespoon of sesame oil and place them on a baking sheet.

3. Bake the tofu and polenta cutlets under the preheated broiler 5 to 6 minutes.
4. Heat the remaining 1 tablespoon of sesame oil in a cast-iron skillet over medium-high heat. Fry the banana slices 5 to 6 minutes.
5. Put the beans into a blender and purée until a thick mixture forms. In a separate bowl, combine the mango, scallions, salt, ground black pepper, paprika, and chili pepper.
6. Place a slice of polenta on a serving plate. Next, place 1/4 of bean mixture on the slice of polenta. Lay a piece of tofu, a few slices of avocado, a few slices of fried banana, and top with 1/4 of the mango salsa. Repeat with remaining ingredients. You will have four serving plates.

Meatless Sizzling Fajitas

(Ready in about 1 hour 15 minutes | Servings 6)

Ingredients

- 1/4 cup canola oil
- 1/4 cup apple cider vinegar
- 1 teaspoon chili powder
- 1 teaspoon garlic powder
- 1 teaspoon dried basil
- 1 teaspoon dried oregano
- 1 teaspoon salt
- 1/4 teaspoon ground white pepper
- 1 small bunch fresh coriander
- 1 teaspoon molasses
- 3 zucchini, julienned
- 1 red bell pepper, sliced
- 1 red onion, chopped
- 2 tablespoons olive oil
- 1 (8.75-ounce) can corn kernels, drained
- 2 cups cooked chickpeas
- 1/2 lime
- 6 warm tortillas

Directions

1. To make the marinade. In a mixing bowl, combine canola oil, vinegar, chili powder, garlic powder, basil, oregano, salt, white pepper, coriander, and molasses.
2. Then, add the zucchini, red bell pepper, and onion. Place the bowl in the refrigerator and marinate veggies for at least 1 hour or overnight.
3. Heat olive oil in a large heavy skillet over medium-high heat. Sauté the marinated veggies until they are tender, approximately 10 minutes.
4. Turn the heat to high, stir in the corn kernels and chickpea, and cook until the vegetables are browned and crisp-tender, for 5 minutes. Squeeze 1/2 of fresh

lime and stir well to combine. Serve with warm tortillas and enjoy!

Potato Curry with Beans

(Ready in about 1 hour | Servings 4)

Ingredients

- 2 potatoes, peeled and cubed
- 2 tablespoons extra-virgin olive oil
- 1/2 cup leeks, diced
- 2 cloves garlic, minced
- 1/2 teaspoon paprika
- 1 teaspoons ground cumin
- 2 teaspoons curry powder
- 1 rounded tablespoon garam masala
- 1 teaspoon sea salt
- 1 cup canned tomatoes
- 2 cups garbanzo beans, rinsed and drained
- 1 cup non-dairy milk

Directions

1. In a pot, place potatoes and cover with salted water. Bring to a boil over high heat. Then, turn the heat to medium-low, cover, and simmer about 15 minutes. Drain the potatoes and allow to steam dry for a few minutes.
2. Warm the olive oil in a skillet over medium heat. Sauté the leeks and garlic until the onion has turned translucent, for 5 minutes.
3. Season with spices and continue cooking for 2 minutes longer. Add the rest of ingredients and simmer on low heat approximately 10 minutes. Serve hot with your favorite salad on the side.

Chickpea Vegetable Stir-Fry

(Ready in about 45 minutes | Servings 4)

Ingredients

- 2 tablespoons peanut oil
- 1 teaspoon dried rosemary
- 1 teaspoon thyme
- 1 teaspoon dried basil
- 1 clove garlic, minced
- 1/2 teaspoon red pepper flakes
- 1/2 teaspoon ground black pepper
- 1 (15 ounce) can chickpeas, drained and rinsed
- 1 large zucchini, sliced
- 1 large carrots, thinly sliced
- 1/2 cup mushrooms, sliced
- 1 tomato, chopped
- 1 tablespoon fresh parsley, roughly chopped

Directions

1. In a wok or a wide saucepan, heat peanut oil over medium heat. Sprinkle with rosemary, thyme, and basil.
2. Add the garlic, red pepper, black pepper, chickpeas, zucchini and carrots, stirring well to combine ingredients. Cover and continue cooking for 8 to 10 minutes.
3. Stir in mushrooms and cook until mushrooms are fragrant and tender, stirring frequently. Lay the chopped tomato on top of the mushroom mixture.
4. Cover with the lid and allow the tomatoes to steam for a few minutes. Sprinkle with fresh parsley and serve immediately.

Perfect Shepherd's Pie
(Ready in about 1 hour 25 minutes | Servings 4)

Ingredients

- 4 white potatoes, peeled and cubed
- 2 tablespoons margarine or nondairy butter
- 1/3 cup unsweetened dairy-free milk
- 1 teaspoon garlic salt, divided
- 1/4 teaspoon ground black pepper
- 1/4 teaspoon red pepper flakes
- 3/4 cup vegan kale pesto
- 2 heaping tablespoons chopped cashews
- 4 cups water
- 1 cup red lentils
- 1 tablespoon margarine or nondairy butter, softened
- 2-3 green onions, sliced
- 1 medium-size carrot, grated
- 1 medium-size zucchini, grated
- 2 plum tomatoes, diced
- 4 leaves fresh basil, minced
- 1 cup soybean cottage cheese
- Nonstick cooking spray

Directions

1. Place the potatoes in a pot, cover with water and bring to a boil. Next, cook approximately 20 minutes or until the potato cubes are fork-tender. Drain.
2. Add margarine or butter, dairy-free milk, 1/2 teaspoon of the garlic salt, black pepper, and red pepper flakes. Mash until the potatoes are smooth. Add the kale pesto and cashews. Stir to combine and set aside.
3. To a deep saucepan, add the water. Add the lentils and cook 15 to 20 minutes, until they are tender. Drain and reserve.
4. In a separate skillet, melt the margarine or butter over medium heat. Sauté the onions, carrot, zucchini,

tomato, and remaining 1/2 teaspoon of garlic salt. Cook until the vegetables turn light brown, about 5 to 6 minutes.
5. Stir in the basil, cooked lentils, and cottage cheese. Simmer additional 2 minutes.
6. Preheat the oven to 375 degrees F. Lightly grease a baking dish with nonstick spray.
7. Place the vegetable and lentil mixture in the bottom of the baking dish. Spread the mashed potato mixture over the top.
8. Cover with an aluminum foil and bake for 20 minutes. Then, remove the foil, and bake for 15 more minutes.
9. Allow the pie to stand for about 15 minutes before cutting and serving.

Flavor-Rich Crusty Tart

(Ready in about 1 hour | Servings 4)

Ingredients

Nonstick cooking spray

For the crust:

- 1 ¼ cups all-purpose flour
- 1/4 teaspoon kosher salt
- 3 tablespoons tahini
- 1/4 cup plus 1 tablespoon water

For the filling:

- 4 cups water
- 1 cup brown lentils
- 1 tablespoon canola oil
- 1 small red onion, finely chopped
- 1 yellow or red bell pepper, thinly sliced
- 2 cloves garlic, minced
- 1 teaspoon kosher salt
- 1/2 teaspoon ground white pepper
- 1 teaspoon ground cumin
- 1/4 teaspoon paprika
- 1/2 teaspoon ground coriander
- 1/2 cup tomato sauce
- 1 tablespoon molasses

Directions

1. Preheat the oven to 375 degrees F. Lightly oil a pie plate with nonstick cooking spray.
2. To make the crust: Mix together the salt, flour and tahini in a food processor or with a mixer. Next, gradually add the water, 1 tablespoon at a time, and mix well to combine.
3. Shape the dough into a disk and roll out the crust. Replace the crust in the oiled pie plate. Gently prick the

crust, for instance with a fork, in order to prevent air bubbles.
4. To make the lentil filling: In a deep and wide saucepan, bring the water to a boil. Next, cook the lentils for about 25 minutes. Drain, and set aside.
5. In a separate saucepan, warm the canola oil over medium heat. Sauté the onion, yellow or red bell pepper and garlic for 4 minutes, or until the vegetables become tender.
6. Season with salt and white pepper. Then, sprinkle with cumin, paprika, and coriander, and continue cooking until fragrant or 1 more minute.
7. Stir in the tomato paste and molasses, and then add cooked lentils. Lower the heat, let simmer for 5 to 7 minutes.
8. Spread the lentil filling over the prepared crust and bake for 40 minutes, or until the filling is set. Allow the tart to rest for about 20 minutes before slicing and serving.

Nutty Mushroom Tofu Casserole

(Ready in about 1 hour 15 minutes | Servings 6)

Ingredients

- 1 (15-ounces) can non-dairy milk
- 1 tablespoon curry powder
- 1 cup button mushrooms, chopped
- 1 ½ cup drained extra-firm tofu, pressed and crumbled
- 2 tablespoons cornstarch
- Nonstick cooking spray
- 2 cups soft wheat flour
- 1 tablespoon fresh parsley, chopped
- 1 tablespoon fresh basil leaves, chopped
- 1 teaspoon onion powder
- 1 teaspoon garlic powder
- 1/2 teaspoon sea salt
- 1/4 teaspoon black pepper
- 1/4 teaspoon cayenne pepper
- 1 tablespoon peanut oil
- 1 onion, chopped
- 1 can white beans, drained and rinsed
- 1/4 cup ground raw pecans
- 1/4 cup nutritional yeast

Directions

1. In a large heavy skillet, bring the milk with curry to a boil. Turn the flame to medium-low and then sauté the mushrooms. Add crumbled tofu and cook on low for 13 to 15 minutes. Then uncover and cook another 10 minutes.
2. Mix cornstarch with 2 tablespoon of cold water in order to make a slurry. Then, gradually add the cornstarch slurry. Mix until it is well combined.
3. Continue cooking until your tofu mixture is thickened or about 5 minutes. Allow this tofu mixture to cool slightly.

4. Preheat the oven to 350 degrees F. Prepare a casserole dish, by spraying lightly with nonstick cooking spray.
5. In a large-size mixing bowl, mix together the flour, parsley, basil, onion powder, garlic powder, sea salt, black pepper, and cayenne pepper.
6. Combine this flour mixture with tofu mixture. Knead the dough and set aside.
7. In a separate skillet, warm the peanut oil and then sauté the onion for a few minutes. Add the beans and cook for 5 to 7 minutes, or until the beans begin to brown.
8. Spread the dough in the bottom of the casserole dish evenly. Place the bean mixture on top of the dough. Scatter the pecans and the nutritional yeast all over the top.
9. Bake, covered with an aluminum foil, for 20 to 25 minutes. Then, remove the foil and bake for 10 more minutes. Allow to rest and cool slightly for about 10 minutes before slicing, and then serve.

Apple Gourmet Sausages
(Ready in about 1 hour 45 minutes | Servings 4)

Ingredients

- 2 cups vital wheat gluten flour
- 1/4 cup nutritional yeast
- 1 teaspoon Himalayan salt
- 1 tablespoon dried basil
- 1 teaspoon onion powder
- 1 teaspoon ground cumin
- 1/2 teaspoon allspice
- 3 tablespoons peanut oil
- 1 ½ tablespoon pure maple syrup
- 1 cup apple juice
- 1 teaspoon lemon zest
- 1 cup unsweetened applesauce

Directions

1. Preheat the oven to 325 degrees F.
2. In a large-size mixing bowl, whisk together the flour, yeast, salt, basil, onion powder, cumin, and allspice.
3. In a separate medium-size bowl, whisk together the rest of ingredients.
4. Combine the dry flour mixture with the wet apple mixture. Stir to combine and then knead for a few minutes with clean hands. Let the dough rest for at least 5 minutes.
5. Roll the dough into 2 logs. Wrap in a foil and bake for 90 minutes. You need to flip the wrapped logs halfway through the cooking time.
6. Cut the sausages into halves and divide among four serving plates. Garnish with fresh sauerkraut and mustard and enjoy!

Amazing Sandwiches with Pumpkin Sausages

(Ready in about 2 hours | Servings 2)

Ingredients

- 1 ½ cups vital wheat gluten flour
- 1/4 cup nutritional yeast
- 1 teaspoon cayenne pepper
- 1 teaspoon dried rosemary
- 1 teaspoon dried basil
- 1 teaspoon dried oregano
- 1/2 teaspoon ground black pepper
- 1/4 teaspoon ground cinnamon
- 1 teaspoon onion powder
- 1 teaspoon garlic powder
- 1 teaspoon agave nectar
- 3/4 cup vegetable stock
- 1/2 cup pumpkin purée
- 2 tablespoons peanut oil
- 2 sandwich buns

Directions

1. Preheat the oven to 325 degrees F. Prepare a baking tray.
2. In a large-size mixing bowl, whisk together the wheat gluten, yeast, cayenne pepper, rosemary, basil, oregano, black pepper, ground cinnamon, onion powder, garlic powder, and agave nectar.
3. In a separate mixing bowl, whisk together the vegetable stock, pumpkin purée, and peanut oil.
4. Pour the pumpkin mixture into the dry mixture, stir well to combine and then knead it for a couple of minutes. Allow to rest for 5 to 10 minutes.
5. Roll the dough into a log. Wrap in a foil and bake for 45 minutes. Then, flip the sausage and continue baking on the other side for another 40 to 45 minutes.

6. Make two sandwiches with vegan buns and enjoy!

Homemade Meatless Frankfurters

(Ready in about 1 hour | Servings 6)

Ingredients

- 1/4 cup nutritional yeast
- 2 cups vital wheat gluten flour
- 1 teaspoon ground cumin
- 1 tablespoon garlic powder
- 1 teaspoon ground black pepper
- 1 tablespoon dried parsley
- 1 teaspoon tarragon
- 1 cup vegetable broth
- 1/2 cup sauerkraut
- 1/4 cup canola oil
- 6 boiled potatoes, for garnish

Directions

1. Preheat the oven to 350 degrees F.
2. In a mixing bowl, combine together the nutritional yeast, wheat gluten, ground cumin, garlic powder, black pepper, dried parsley, and tarragon.
3. In a separate mixing bowl, whisk together the vegetable broth, sauerkraut, and canola oil.
4. Next, combine the dry mixture with wet mixture and mix until everything is well combined.
5. Divide the batter into 12 equal pieces. Then, shape each piece into Vienna-style sausage. Wrap in an aluminum foil and bake for about 40 minutes.
6. Serve with boiled potatoes. You can serve as a hot dog.

Savory Vegetable Muffins

(Ready in about 45 minutes | Servings 6)

Ingredients

- Nonstick cooking spray
- 2 teaspoons white vinegar
- 1 ½ cups unsweetened soy milk
- 3 tablespoons ground flax seed
- 1/4 cup water
- 1 cup cornmeal
- 2 cups all-purpose flour
- 1 teaspoon kosher salt
- 1 teaspoon baking soda
- 1/4 cup olive oil
- 1 teaspoon ground cumin
- 1 teaspoon onion powder
- 8 sun-dried tomatoes in oil, drained and chopped
- 1 yellow bell pepper, chopped
- 1 red bell pepper, chopped
- 4 small pickles, finely chopped

Directions

1. Preheat the oven to 350 degrees F. Lightly oil a 12-cup muffin pan with spray.
2. In a mixing bowl, mix together the white vinegar and soy milk.
3. In a separate small-size bowl, combine the flax seeds with water.
4. In a separate large-size bowl, whisk together the cornmeal, flour, salt, and baking soda.
5. Add the flaxseed mixture to the soymilk mixture, along with the olive oil, cumin, and onion powder. Fold this mixture into the flour mixture, and gently stir to combine. Next, fold in the tomatoes, bell peppers, and pickles.

6. Divide the batter equally among 12 muffin cups and bake until a toothpick inserted into the center of the muffin comes out clean, or for 18 to 20 minutes.
7. Transfer the muffins to a wire rack to cool before serving.

Creamy Bean and Tomato Soup

(Ready in about 45 minutes | Servings 6)

Ingredients

- 1 tablespoon canola oil
- 1 red onion, finely chopped
- 1 teaspoon garlic powder
- 1 teaspoon dried rosemary
- 2 carrots, chopped
- 1 stalk celery, chopped
- 2 tablespoons chili powder
- 1 tablespoon marjoram
- Sea salt to taste
- 1/2 teaspoon black pepper
- 4 cups vegetable broth
- 4 (15-ounce) cans black beans
- 1 (14.5-ounce) can crushed tomatoes

Directions

1. Heat canola oil in a large stockpot over medium-high flame. Add onion, garlic powder, rosemary, carrots and celery, and cook for 5 minutes. Season with chili powder, marjoram, salt and black pepper. Continue cooking for 1 minute longer.
2. Pour in vegetable broth, and then fold in 2 cans of beans. Bring to a boil.
3. In a food processor or blender, process remaining 2 cans of beans with crushed tomatoes until uniform and smooth.
4. Stir this mixture into boiling soup mixture, turn the heat to medium, and simmer for about 15 minutes. Serve hot with your favorite vegan croutons.

Saucy Tofu with Vegetables

(Ready in about 20 minutes | Servings 4)

Ingredients

- 1 tablespoon walnut oil
- 1/2 small head cauliflower, broken into small florets
- 1 small head broccoli, broken into small florets
- 1 green bell pepper, chopped
- 5 fresh mushrooms, sliced
- 1 pound firm tofu, cubed
- 1/2 cup nut butter
- 1/2 cup hot water
- 2 tablespoons tamari sauce
- 1 tablespoon pure maple syrup
- 1/2 teaspoon sea salt
- 1/2 teaspoon red pepper flakes
- 1/2 teaspoon paprika

Directions

1. In a wide heavy skillet, heat walnut oil over medium-high heat. Sauté cauliflower, broccoli, bell pepper, mushrooms and tofu for 5 to 7 minutes.
2. In a small mixing bowl, combine butter, hot water, tamari sauce, maple syrup, salt, red pepper and paprika.
3. Pour this mixture over vegetables and tofu in the skillet. Cook on low heat for 3 to 5 minutes, until the vegetables are tender and crisp.

Mushroom and Carrot Stuffed Zucchini

(Ready in about 1 hour | Servings 8)

Ingredients

- Nonstick cooking spray
- 4 medium-size zucchini, unpeeled and halved
- 1 tablespoon walnut oil
- 4 green onions, chopped
- 2 cloves garlic, minced
- 2 large-size carrots, grated
- 1 cup mushrooms, sliced
- 1 teaspoon ground cumin
- 1 (15-ounce) can white beans, rinsed and drained
- 2 tablespoons apple cider vinegar
- 2 tablespoons chopped fresh parsley
- 1/4 teaspoon grated nutmeg
- 1 teaspoon sea salt
- 1/4 teaspoon ground black pepper
- 1/4 teaspoon cayenne pepper

Directions

1. Preheat the oven to 350 degrees F. Oil a shallow casserole or baking dish with nonstick cooking spray.
2. To prepare the zucchini "boats": Scoop out the flesh of the zucchini. Chop the zucchini flesh and set aside. Place the boats in the greased baking dish.
3. To make the filling. Heat walnut oil in a wide saucepan over medium heat. Sauté green onions for 5 minutes. Stir in minced garlic and sauté 2 minutes more, until it is lightly browned and fragrant.
4. Stir in the chopped flesh of the zucchini, carrots and mushrooms, and cook 5 minutes. Stir in remaining ingredients and cook a couple of minutes. Stuff the zucchini boats with prepared mushroom filling.
5. Bake until stuffed zucchini boats become soft, for about 40 minutes.

Mexican-Style Macaroni Skillet

(Ready in about 25 minutes | Servings 4)

Ingredients

- 1/2 pound eggless macaroni
- 2 tablespoons canola oil
- 3 spring onions, chopped
- 1 red or green bell pepper, chopped
- 1 (15.5-ounce) can chickpeas, drained
- 1 (14.5-ounce) can diced tomatoes
- 1 tablespoon fresh parsley, chopped
- 1 tablespoon white wine
- 1/2 cup corn kernels
- 1/4 cup olives, sliced
- 1/2 teaspoon kosher salt
- 1/4 teaspoon cayenne pepper
- 1/4 teaspoon ground black pepper
- 1/4 cup salsa

Directions

1. Bring a pot of salted water to a boil and cook the macaroni for about 10 minutes or until al dente.
2. Meanwhile, in a heavy skillet, warm canola oil over medium-high heat. Sauté spring onions and bell pepper until the vegetables are tender and lightly browned, for 10 minutes.
3. Stir in chickpeas, tomatoes, parsley, wine, corn kernels, olives, salt, cayenne pepper, black pepper and salsa. Cook until your sauce is thoroughly heated, or 5 to 7 minutes.
4. Toss the sauce with the macaroni and serve with some extra olives and your favorite salad.

Herbed and Stewed Summer Vegetables

(Ready in about 25 minutes | Servings 4)

Ingredients

- 1/2 cup extra-virgin olive oil
- 2 shallots, thinly sliced
- 2 cloves garlic, minced
- 2 zucchini, peeled and diced
- 1 stalk celery, chopped
- 1 large-size carrot, sliced
- 1 medium eggplant, cubed
- 1 yellow squash, cubed
- 2 red bell peppers, chopped
- 1 jalapeño pepper, minced
- 4 medium-size tomatoes, peeled and diced
- 1 tablespoon fresh parsley, roughly chopped
- 1 tablespoon fresh cilantro, roughly chopped
- 1 teaspoon sea salt
- 1/2 teaspoon black pepper
- 1/2 teaspoon paprika

Directions

1. In a large pot over medium-low heat, cook the shallots and garlic in 1 ½ tablespoon of hot olive oil. Cook until tender and translucent.
2. In a wok or a wide skillet, heat 1 ½ tablespoon of olive oil and sauté the zucchini until they are slightly browned. Add the zucchini to the pot with the shallots and garlic.
3. Add remaining olive oil and add celery, carrot, eggplant, squash, bell peppers, and jalapeño pepper. Cook over medium heat for 20 minutes longer. Replace to the pot.
4. Add the tomatoes to the pot, sprinkle with herbs and spices and cook another 12 to 15 minutes, stirring occasionally. Taste, adjust the seasonings and serve hot.

Tangy BBQ Sandwiches with Tempeh
(Ready in about 25 minutes | Servings 4)

Ingredients

- 1 cup vegan BBQ sauce
- 1 cup tempeh, crumbled
- 1 tablespoon extra-virgin olive oil
- 1 medium leek, finely chopped
- 1 large-size carrot, cut into strips
- 2 red or green bell peppers, thinly sliced
- 4 sandwich rolls, split
- 1 teaspoon mustard
- 8-10 iceberg lettuce leaves, drizzled with lemon juice

Directions

1. Into a medium-size bowl, pour the BBQ sauce of your choice. Place the tempeh in the bowl, and let it marinate about 10 to 15 minutes.
2. Heat olive oil in a cast-iron skillet over medium heat. Add the leek, carrot, and sliced bell peppers.
3. Cook, stirring often, until the vegetables are tender. Stir in the marinated tempeh together with sauce, and cook until it is heated through.
4. Spoon the tempeh with vegetables onto sandwich rolls, garnish with mustard and iceberg lettuce and serve.

Colorful Mushroom Vegetable Pilaf
(Ready in about 40 minutes | Servings 8)

Ingredients

- 1 tablespoon canola oil
- 4 spring onions, chopped
- 4 cloves garlic, minced
- 1 cup quinoa, rinsed
- 1 cup half cooked wild rice
- 1 cup canned lentils, rinsed
- 2 medium-size carrots
- 2 stalks celery, chopped
- 1 cup fresh mushrooms, chopped
- 1 quart vegetable broth
- 1 teaspoon dried basil
- 1 teaspoon dried rosemary
- 1 bunch kale, stems removed
- 1 teaspoon fine sea salt
- 1/4 teaspoon ground white pepper
- 1/4 teaspoon cayenne pepper
- 1 tablespoon fresh parsley, chopped

Directions

1. In a large-size pot, warm canola oil over medium heat. Stir in the spring onions and garlic, and sauté 5 minutes, until spring onions are translucent and tender.
2. Stir in quinoa, wild rice, lentils, carrots, celery, and mushrooms. Pour in the vegetable broth, cover with the lid and cook for about 10 minutes. Season with basil and rosemary and continue cooking another 10 minutes.
3. Turn off the stove and add remaining ingredients to the pot. Place the lid, and allow to stand for 8 to 10 minutes, until kale is wilted.

Mediterranean Veggie Couscous
(Ready in about 40 minutes | Servings 8)

Ingredients

- 1 cup water
- 1 cup sun-dried tomatoes, dehydrated
- 1/2 (10-ounce) package couscous
- 1 teaspoon sesame oil
- 3 cloves garlic, pressed
- 1 large red onion, finely chopped
- 1 carrot, shredded
- 1/3 cup fresh basil leaves
- Juice of 1/2 fresh lemon
- 1/2 teaspoon sea salt
- 1/4 teaspoon black pepper
- 1/4 teaspoon cayenne pepper
- 1/2 cup mushroom, sliced
- Sliced olives for garnish

Directions

1. Pour the water into a bowl. Then place the sun-dried tomatoes in a bowl and soak them for 30 minutes. Remove rehydrated tomatoes from the water, drain and chop them. Reserve the tomato water.
2. In a deep saucepan, combine the reserved tomato water with 1/2 cup of water. Bring to a boil and cook the couscous. Remove from the flame and allow to sit for 5 minutes, until liquid has been absorbed. Then fluff the couscous with a fork.
3. In a heavy skillet, heat the sesame oil over medium heat. Next, stir in the reserved and rehydrated sun-dried tomatoes, garlic, and red onion.
4. Cook about 5 minutes, stirring frequently, until the onions are translucent, fragrant and tender. Mix in the carrot, basil, and lemon juice. Season with sea salt, black pepper, and cayenne.

5. Stir in the mushrooms, and continue cooking for 5 minutes. Stir occasionally. Toss this mixture with the couscous, taste, adjust the seasonings and transfer to the serving platter. Garnish with olives and serve immediately.

Easy Portobello Mushroom Pasta

(Ready in about 30 minutes | Servings 4)

Ingredients

- 5 tablespoons canola oil
- 1 small bunch spring onions, chopped
- 4 cloves garlic, minced
- 4 Roma tomatoes, diced
- 1 large-size carrot, thinly sliced
- 1 cup Portobello mushrooms, sliced
- 1 teaspoon dried basil
- 1/2 teaspoon dried oregano
- 1 teaspoon dried rosemary
- 1 tablespoon cilantro
- 1 teaspoon sea salt
- 1/4 teaspoon black pepper
- 1/4 teaspoon paprika
- 1 pound eggless pasta of choice

Directions

1. In a medium-size heavy skillet, heat the oil over medium-high heat. Then sauté spring onions and garlic for 2 to 4 minutes, until they are just tender and fragrant.
2. Stir in tomatoes, carrot and mushrooms, and cook 5 minutes until the carrot becomes slightly soft. Next, sprinkle with basil, oregano, rosemary, cilantro, sea salt, black pepper, and paprika.
3. Next, reduce the heat to low and let simmer for 10 minutes longer.
4. Bring a pot of lightly salted water to a boil and cook your favorite pasta. Cook approximately 5 minutes, until al dente.
5. Toss drained pasta with sauce and divide among four serving plates. You can garnish with crumbled tofu, olives, ketchup, it's up to you.

Super Healthy Vegetable Rice Stew

(Ready in about 1 hour 30 minutes | Servings 4)

Ingredients

- 1 eggplant, peeled and sliced
- 1 teaspoon sea salt
- 1/4 cup canola oil
- 1 cup leeks, chopped
- 4 cloves garlic, crushed
- 1/2 cup brown rice
- 1 green bell pepper, thinly sliced
- 1 red bell pepper, thinly sliced
- 3 fresh tomatoes, diced
- 1 ½ cups water
- 2 tablespoons sherry vinegar
- 1/2 teaspoon salt
- 1/4 teaspoon ground black pepper
- 1/4 teaspoon red pepper flakes
- 1/4 cup fresh basil leaves, chopped
- 1 sprig fresh rosemary, chopped
- 1 tablespoon fresh cilantro, chopped
- 1 tablespoon fresh parsley, chopped
- 1 bay leaf

Directions

1. Sprinkle the slices of eggplant with 1 teaspoon of salt. Place slices of eggplant in a colander and allow to stand for about 30 minutes. Rinse the slices of eggplant and pat dry.
2. Heat canola oil in a large pot over medium heat. Sauté eggplant until slightly browned. Then, add leeks and sauté until fragrant and tender, for 5 minutes. Add the garlic and sauté for 2 to 3 minutes longer.
3. Stir in brown rice, green bell pepper, red bell pepper, tomatoes, water, sherry vinegar, salt, black pepper, and red pepper flakes. Turn the heat to medium-high and

cook for about 10 minutes. Turn the heat to medium-low and simmer for 45 minutes, or until vegetables become soft.
4. Remove the pot from the heat and stir in basil, rosemary, cilantro, parsley, and bay leaf. Enjoy immediately!

Peppery Seitan Fajitas

(Ready in about 30 minutes | Servings 5)

Ingredients

- 2 tablespoons extra-virgin olive oil
- 1 small onion, finely chopped
- 2 red bell pepper, thinly sliced
- 1 green bell pepper, thinly sliced
- 1 jalapeño pepper, seeded and minced
- 1 pound seitan, cut into strips
- 2 tablespoons tamari sauce
- 3 cloves garlic, minced
- 1 teaspoon smoked paprika
- 1/4 teaspoon ground black pepper
- 1 teaspoon turmeric
- 1 teaspoon ground cumin
- 1/2 teaspoon kosher salt
- 10 whole grain vegan tortillas

Directions

1. To make the filling: Heat olive oil in a large heavy skillet over medium heat. Cook the onion, bell peppers, and jalapeño pepper, until they become tender, about 5 minutes.
2. Add seitan, tamari sauce, garlic, smoked paprika, black pepper, turmeric, and ground cumin. Turn the heat to low. Season with salt and continue cooking for 10 minutes longer.
3. Warm the tortillas. Spoon seitan filling onto each tortilla and fold the tortillas.

Free Ebook Offer

The Ultimate Guide To Vitamins
I'm very excited to be able to make this offer to you. This is a wonderful 10k word ebook that has been made available to you through my publisher, Valerian Press. As a health conscious person you should be well aware of the uses and health benefits of each of the vitamins that should make up our diet. This book gives you an easy to understand, scientific explanation of the vitamin followed by the recommended daily dosage. It then highlights all the important health benefits of each vitamin. A list of the best sources of each vitamin is provided and you are also given some actionable next steps for each vitamin to make sure you are utilizing the information!

As well as receiving the free ebooks you will also be sent a weekly stream of free ebooks, again from my publishing company Valerian Press. You can expect to receive at least a new, free ebook each and every week. Sometimes you might receive a massive 10 free books in a week!

All you need to do is type this link into your browser:
http://bit.ly/18hmup4

About the Author

Hello! I'm Jessica Brooks, relatively new to the world of authorship but a veteran of the health and diet industry. If you have read any of my books, I would like to thank you from the bottom of my heart. I truly hope they have helped answer your questions and injected some inspiration into your life. Thanks to my wonderful upbringing I have been a vegetarian since infancy, making to jump to veganism nearly 20 years ago. I'm passionate about helping people improve their health! Over the coming months I am hoping to write a couple more books that will help people learn, start and succeed with certain diets.

In my spare time I am an avid reader of fantasy fiction (George Martin, you demon!). You can often find me lounging in my hammock with my latest book well into the evening. Outside of reading, I love all things physical. From hiking to sailing, swimming to skiing I'm a fan of it all! I try to practice Yoga a couple of times a week, I really recommend everyone gives it a try. You will just feel amazing after a good session!

You can find a facebook page I help manage here:

https://www.facebook.com/CleanFoodDiet

I would like to thank my publishers Valerian Press for giving me the opportunity to create this book.

Valerian Press

At Valerian Press we have three key beliefs.

Providing outstanding value: We believe in enriching all of our customers' lives, doing everything we can to ensure the best experience.

Championing new talent: We believe in showcasing the worlds emerging talent by giving them the platform to grow.

Simplicity and efficiency: We understand how valuable your time is. Our products are stream-lined and consist only of what you want. You will find no fluff with us.

We hope you have enjoyed reading Jessica's guide to the vegan diet.

We would love to offer you a regular supply of our free and discounted books. We cover a huge range of non-fiction genres; diet and cookbooks, health and fitness, alternative and holistic medicine, spirituality and plenty more. All you need to do is type this link into your web browser: http://bit.ly/18hmup4

Free Preview of "Vegan Slow Cooker Cookbook: 100 Delicious Recipes"

Tempeh chili with Vaquero beans

It's a protein packed dish for a healthy meal. Serve it over rice or quinoa for a hearty lunch or dinner.

Serves: 6

Ingredients:

- Olive oil – 2 tablespoons
- Onion – ½ small, minced
- Garlic – 3 cloves, minced
- Soy tempeh – 8 ounces, diced
- Cooked Vaquero beans – 6 cups or Pinto beans – 3 cans, rinsed and drained
- Water – 4 cups
- Tomatoes – 1 can, diced
- Tomato paste – 1 tablespoon
- Chili powder – 1 teaspoon
- Pasilla chile powder – 1 teaspoon
- Oregano – 1 teaspoon
- Paprika – 1/2 teaspoon
- Chipotle powder – ¼-1/2 teaspoon
- Plain or smoked salt, to taste
- Cashew cream or vegan sour cream, for serving

Method

In a pan, heat olive oil and sauté onion until tender and translucent. Then add garlic and again stir fry for a few minutes. Remove from the pan. With all the other ingredients except sour cream, put onion-garlic in a slow cooker. Turn on the cooker on high and cook for 4-5 hours.

While serving, top it up with a little sour cream and enjoy!

Vegan Slow cooker Cincinnati Chili

It's a great spaghetti topping for a wholesome meal. Enjoy it either in lunch or at dinner or amuse your guests with its amazing flavors!

Note: Prepare the chili a day before if you want to devour it for lunch.

Serves: 2

Ingredients:

For morning

- Dry black beluga lentils – ¾ cup (use any other lentil if you do not want dark color chili)
- Water – 1 ½ cups
- Garlic – 2 cloves, minced
- Bay leaf – 1
- Grounded vegan crumbles – ½ cup (if you want a soy free version, then use cooked quinoa – ½ cup)
- Ground cumin – 1/2 teaspoon
- Ground hot pepper (any) – ¼ teaspoon
- Ground cinnamon – 1/8 teaspoon
- Chili powder – 1 teaspoon
- Cocoa powder – 1 teaspoon
- Ground allspice – 1 pinch

For evening

- Tomatoes – 1 ½ cups, diced
- Fresh ground nutmeg – a dash
- Salt, to taste
- Cooked pasta – 2-3 cups (for serving)

Method

In the morning, add all the morning ingredients in a 1 ½- 2 quart slow cooker and cook on low for 7-9 hours.

Half an hour before serving, open the cooker and add tomatoes, salt and nutmeg. Cook on high until the tomatoes get smashed and mixed with other ingredients.

Serve hot over cooked pasta and top it up with chopped onions or shredded vegan cheese or cooked beans, all optional though.

Grains and beans slow cooker chili

Chili can never go wrong as a main dish. It works well if you are in a mood to have a family get together or are planning for a formal event. Top it over cooked rice or pasta or simply eat with a taco or quesadillas, you'll love it all the time!

Serves: 3-4

Ingredients:

- Assorted dry beans (no kidney beans) – 2 cups
- Water – 6 cups
- Tomato puree or diced tomatoes – 1 can
- Millet – 1/8 cup
- Dry vegan bouillon – 1 tablespoon
- Cumin – 1 teaspoon
- Chili spice mix – 1 teaspoon
- Ancho powder or chipotle – ½ teaspoon
- Smoked paprika – ½ teaspoon
- Salt, to taste

Method

In a 1-1 ½ quart slow cooker, add beans and 4 cups water at night. Cook for 7-9 hours or overnight on low temperature.

In the morning, remove the beans from the cooker and rinse them. Again add beans with all other ingredients and 2 cups water. Add salt before serving. Now let everything cook on low for 7-10 hours.

Crockpot vegan bean chili with steel-cut oats

Chili is for all seasons and this one is a perfect main dish to be served over cooked quinoa or rice.

Serves: 6

Ingredients:

- Water – 6 cups
- Veggie bouillon – 2 cubes
- Steel-cut oats – 1/2 cup
- Oregano – 1 tablespoon
- Ground cumin – 2 teaspoons
- Chili powder – 1 teaspoon
- Garlic – 3 cloves, minced
- Kidney beans – 1-14.5 ounces can, drained and rinsed
- Black beans - 1-14.5 ounces can, drained and rinsed
- Tomatoes - 1-14.5 ounces can, diced
- Fire-roasted or regular frozen corns – 1 cup
- Liquid smoke, to taste
- ½ lime juice
- Salt and pepper, to taste

Method

In a 1-1 ½ quart slow cooker, add everything except lime juice and salt & pepper.

Cook for 7-10 hours on low heat. Before serving, add salt & pepper and squeeze ½ lime over chili.

To grab this exciting vegan/vegetarian cookbook be sure to type this link into your web browser:
http://www.amazon.com/dp/B00W0F05JE

Or search for Jessica Brooks on amazon!

Printed in Great Britain
by Amazon